MW00677880

To:

_____

From:

_____

Date:

_____

Promises from God for Mothers

© 2015 Christian Art Gifts, RSA
Christian Art Gifts Inc., IL, USA

First edition 2015

Designed by Christian Art Gifts

Images used under license from Shutterstock.com

Printed in China

ISBN 978-1-4321-2184-6 – LuxLeather
ISBN 978-1-4321-2190-7 – Hardcover

Christian Art Gifts has made every effort to trace the
ownership of all quotes and poems in this book. In the event of
any question that may arise from the use of any quote or poem, we
regret any error made and will be pleased to make the necessary
correction in future editions of this book.

15 16 17 18 19 20 21 22 23 24 – 10 9 8 7 6 5 4 3 2 1

Promises from God
for Mothers

christian
art gifts®

In God's promises we will always find ...

God assures us of ...

As for me and my household we will ...

For God's faithful promises we ...

A mother's prayers ...

Guidance for our path

The LORD will guide you always;
He will satisfy your needs in a
sun-scorched land and will
strengthen your frame. You will be
like a well-watered garden, like
a spring whose waters never fail.

Isaiah 58:11 NIV

Whether you turn to the right
or to the left, your ears will hear
a voice behind you, saying,
"This is the way; walk in it."

Isaiah 30:21 NIV

In all your ways acknowledge Him,
and He shall direct your paths.

Proverbs 3:6 NKJV

The LORD directs our steps.

Proverbs 20:24 NLT

The LORD is good and does what
is right; He shows the proper
path to those who go astray.
He leads the humble in doing
right, teaching them His way.

Psalm 25:8-9 NLT

God is our God for ever
and ever; He will be our
Guide even to the end.

Psalm 48:14 NIV

Put your hope in the LORD.
Travel steadily along His path.

Psalm 37:34 NLT

The Lord replied,
"My Presence will go with you,
and I will give you rest."

Exodus 33:14 NIV

The Lord makes firm the
steps of the one who delights
in Him; though he may stumble,
he will not fall, for the Lord
upholds him with His hand.

Psalm 37:23-24 NIV

The Lord says, "I will go before
you and make the crooked
places straight; I will break
in pieces the gates of bronze
and cut the bars of iron."

Isaiah 45:2 NKJV

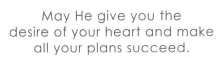

May He give you the
desire of your heart and make
all your plans succeed.

Psalm 20:4 NIV

The LORD says, "I will guide
you along the best pathway
for your life. I will advise you
and watch over you."

Psalm 32:8 NLT

All who are led by the Spirit of
God are children of God.

Romans 8:14 NLT

Jesus answered, "I am the
way and the truth and the life.
No one comes to the Father
except through Me."

John 14:6 NIV

Your Word is a lamp for my feet, a light on my path.

Psalm 119:105 NIV

In God's promises we will always find ...

Strength for each day

Don't be dejected and sad, for the
joy of the LORD is your strength!

Nehemiah 8:10 NLT

God is our refuge and
strength, an ever-present
help in trouble. Therefore we
will not fear, though the earth
give way and the mountains
fall into the heart of the sea.

Psalm 46:1-2 NIV

I can do all things through
Christ who strengthens me.

Philippians 4:13 NKJV

The Sovereign Lord is my
strength; He makes my feet like
the feet of a deer, He enables
me to tread on the heights.

Habakkuk 3:19 NIV

He said, "My grace is sufficient
for you, for My strength is
made perfect in weakness."

2 Corinthians 12:9 NKJV

The Lord is faithful, and He
will strengthen and protect
you from the evil one.

2 Thessalonians 3:3 NIV

"Do not fear, for I am with you;
do not be dismayed, for I am
your God. I will strengthen you
and help you; I will uphold you
with My righteous right hand."

Isaiah 41:10 NIV

The God of Israel gives
power and strength to His
people. Praise be to God!

Psalm 68:35 NLT

"I will seek the lost, and I will bring back the strayed, and I will bind up the injured, and I will strengthen the weak."

Ezekiel 34:16 ESV

Be strong in the Lord and in His mighty power. Put on the full armor of God, so that you can take your stand against the devil's schemes.

Ephesians 6:10 NIV

The LORD is my strength and shield. I trust Him with all my heart. He helps me, and my heart is filled with joy. The LORD gives His people strength. He is a safe fortress for His anointed.

Psalm 28:7-8 NLT

In Your strength I can crush an army;
with my God I can scale any wall.

Psalm 18:29 NLT

God arms me with strength,
and He makes my way perfect.
He makes me as surefooted as
a deer, enabling me to stand on
mountain heights. He trains my
hands for battle; He strengthens
my arm to draw a bronze bow.

Psalm 18:32-34 NLT

The LORD gives power to the weak
and strength to the powerless.

Isaiah 40:29 NLT

The Lord
gives strength to
His people; the
Lord blesses His
people with peace.

Psalm 29:11 NIV

Words of encouragement

"Be strong and courageous!
Do not be afraid or discouraged.
For the LORD your God is with
you wherever you go."

Joshua 1:9 NLT

You, LORD, hear the desire of
the afflicted; You encourage
them, and You listen to their
cry, defending the fatherless
and the oppressed.

Psalm 10:17-18 NIV

The Scriptures give us hope and
encouragement as we wait
patiently for God's promises to be
fulfilled. May God, who gives this
patience and encouragement,
help you live in complete
harmony with each other.

Romans 15:4-5 NLT

17

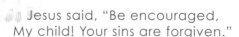

Jesus said, "Be encouraged,
My child! Your sins are forgiven."

Matthew 9:2 NLT

God has not given us a spirit
of fear, but of power and of
love and of a sound mind.

2 Timothy 1:7 NKJV

May our Lord Jesus Christ
Himself and God our Father,
who loved us and by His grace
gave us eternal encouragement
and good hope, encourage
your hearts and strengthen you
in every good deed and word.

2 Thessalonians 2:16-17 NIV

"Do not be afraid of them, for
I am with you and will rescue
you," declares the LORD.

Jeremiah 1:8 NIV

The humble will see their
God at work and be glad.
Let all who seek God's help
be encouraged. For the LORD
hears the cries of the needy.

Psalm 69:32-33 NLT

As soon as I pray, You
answer me; You encourage
me by giving me strength.

Psalm 138:3 NLT

Encourage each other
and build each other up,
just as you are already doing.

1 Thessalonians 5:11 NLT

Your words have supported those
who were falling; You encouraged
those with shaky knees.

Job 4:4 NLT

Be strong and courageous;
do not be afraid or lose heart!

1 Chronicles 22:13 NLT

Because God wanted to make
the unchanging nature of His
purpose very clear, He confirmed
it with an oath. God did this so that
we may be greatly encouraged.

Hebrews 6:17-18 NIV

Be of good courage, and He
shall strengthen your heart, all
you who hope in the LORD.

Psalm 31:24 NKJV

Worry weighs a person down; an encouraging word cheers a person up.

Proverbs 12:25 NLT

Assurance in Christ

Let us hold fast the confession
of our hope without wavering,
for He who promised is faithful.

Hebrews 10:23 ESV

The faithful love of the LORD
never ends! His mercies
never cease. Great is His
faithfulness; His mercies
begin afresh each morning.

Lamentations 3:22-23 NLT

He will keep you strong to
the end so that you will be
free from all blame on the day
when our LORD Jesus Christ returns.
God will do this, for He is faithful
to do what He says, and He has
invited you into partnership with
His Son, Jesus Christ our LORD.

1 Corinthians 1:8-9 NLT

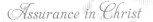

"Heaven and earth will pass
away, but My words will
by no means pass away."

Matthew 24:35 NKJV

If we are unfaithful, He
remains faithful, for He
cannot deny who He is.

2 Timothy 2:13 NLT

Know that the Lord your God,
He is God, the faithful God who
keeps covenant and mercy for
a thousand generations with
those who love Him and keep
His commandments.

Deuteronomy 7:9 NKJV

By this we shall know that we are of the truth and reassure our heart before Him; God is greater than our heart, and He knows everything. We have confidence before God; and whatever we ask we receive from Him, because we keep His commandments and do what pleases Him.

1 John 3:19-22 ESV

To all who did receive Him, who believed in His name, He gave the right to become children of God.

John 1:12 ESV

The righteous will never be shaken; they will be remembered forever. They will have no fear of bad news; their hearts are steadfast, trusting in the Lord.

Psalm 112:6-7 NIV

24

"Most assuredly, I say to you, whatever you ask the Father in My name He will give you."

John 16:23 NKJV

He is the L ORD our God. He remembers His covenant forever, the promise He made, for a thousand generations.

Psalm 105:7-8 NIV

"I have come that they may have life, and have it to the full."

John 10:10 NIV

The L ORD is righteous in all His ways and faithful in all He does.

Psalm 145:17 NIV

Surely goodness
and mercy shall follow
me all the days of my
life; and I will dwell
in the house of the
Lord forever.

Psalm 23:6 NKJV

In God's promises we will always find ...

Rest for our souls

In peace I will lie down and
sleep, for You alone, Lord,
make me dwell in safety.

Psalm 4:8 NIV

Cast your cares on the Lord and
He will sustain you; He will never
let the righteous be shaken.

Psalm 55:22 NIV

Anyone who enters God's
rest also rests from their works,
just as God did from His.

Hebrews 4:10 NIV

He makes me lie down in
green pastures, He leads
me beside quiet waters,
He refreshes my soul.

Psalm 23:2-3 NIV

Whoever dwells in the shelter
of the Most High will rest in
the shadow of the Almighty.

Psalm 91:1 NIV

Truly my soul finds rest in
God; my salvation comes
from Him. Truly He is my rock
and my salvation; He is my
fortress, I will never be shaken.

Psalm 62:1-2 NIV

"Peace I leave with you;
My peace I give you. Do not
let your hearts be troubled
and do not be afraid."

John 14:27 NIV

Rest in the LORD, and wait
patiently for Him; do not
fret because of him who
prospers in his way, because
of the man who brings
wicked schemes to pass.

Psalm 37:7 NKJV

"I will refresh the weary
and satisfy the faint."

Jeremiah 31:25 NIV

Jesus said, "Come to Me, all of
you who are weary and carry
heavy burdens, and I will give
you rest. Take My yoke upon you.
Let Me teach you, because I am
humble and gentle at heart, and
you will find rest for your souls.
For My yoke is easy to bear, and
the burden I give you is light."

Matthew 11:28-30 NLT

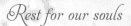

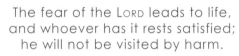

The fear of the LORD leads to life,
and whoever has it rests satisfied;
he will not be visited by harm.

Proverbs 19:23 ESV

It is useless for you to work
so hard from early morning
until late at night, anxiously
working for food to eat; for God
gives rest to His loved ones.

Psalm 127:2 NLT

The eternal God is your
refuge, and His everlasting
arms are under you.

Deuteronomy 33:27 NLT

Therefore,
if anyone is in Christ,
he is a new creation;
old things have passed
away; behold, all things
have become new.

2 Corinthians 5:17 NKJV

In God's promises we will always find ...

Comfort for
our weary hearts

This is what the LORD says:
"As a mother comforts her
child, so will I comfort you."

Isaiah 66:12-13 NIV

Shout for joy, you heavens;
rejoice, you earth; burst into
song, you mountains! For the LORD
comforts His people and will have
compassion on His afflicted ones.

Isaiah 49:13 NIV

All praise to God, the Father of
our Lord Jesus Christ. God is our
merciful Father and the source
of all comfort. He comforts us in
all our troubles so that we can
comfort others. When they are
troubled, we will be able to give
them the same comfort God has
given us. For the more we suffer
for Christ, the more God will shower
us with His comfort through Christ.

2 Corinthians 1:3-5 NLT

I cried out, "I am slipping!"
but Your unfailing love, O Lord,
supported me. When doubts filled
my mind, Your comfort gave
me renewed hope and cheer.

Psalm 94:18-19 NLT

"Blessed are those who mourn,
for they will be comforted."

Matthew 5:4 NIV

"I, yes I, am the One who comforts
you. So why are you afraid?"

Isaiah 51:12 NLT

"I have told you these things,
so that in Me you may have
peace. In this world you will
have trouble. But take heart!
I have overcome the world."

John 16:33 NIV

The Lord is close to the
brokenhearted; He rescues
those whose spirits are crushed.

Psalm 34:18 NLT

The Lord upholds all
who fall, and raises up all
who are bowed down.

Psalm 145:14 NKJV

Even when I walk through
the darkest valley, I will not
be afraid, for You are close
beside me. Your rod and Your
staff protect and comfort me.

Psalm 23:4 NLT

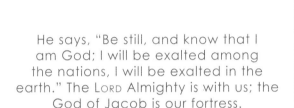

He says, "Be still, and know that I am God; I will be exalted among the nations, I will be exalted in the earth." The LORD Almighty is with us; the God of Jacob is our fortress.

Psalm 46:10-11 NIV

The LORD heals the brokenhearted and binds up their wounds.

Psalm 147:3 NIV

May Your unfailing love be my comfort, according to Your promise.

Psalm 119:76 NIV

"I will turn their mourning into joy. I will comfort them and exchange their sorrow for rejoicing."

Jeremiah 31:13 NLT

God assures us of ...

Fountains of joy

You make known to me the
path of life; You will fill me with
joy in Your presence, with eternal
pleasures at Your right hand.

Psalm 16:11 NIV

You will go out in joy and
be led forth in peace;
the mountains and hills will
burst into song before you,
and all the trees of the
field will clap their hands.

Isaiah 55:12 NIV

Those who sow with tears
will reap with songs of joy.
Those who go out weeping,
carrying seed to sow, will
return with songs of joy,
carrying sheaves with them.

Psalm 126:5-6 NIV

The Lord says, "Be happy!
Yes, leap for joy! For a great
reward awaits you in heaven."

Luke 6:23 NLT

You make me glad by Your
deeds, Lord; I sing for joy at
what Your hands have done.

Psalm 92:4 NIV

Those who look to Him for help
will be radiant with joy; no shadow
of shame will darken their faces.

Psalm 34:5 NLT

Be truly glad. There is
wonderful joy ahead, even
though you must endure
many trials for a little while.

1 Peter 1:6 NLT

He will yet fill your mouth with laughing, and your lips with rejoicing.

Job 8:21 NKJV

His anger lasts only a moment, but His favor lasts a lifetime! Weeping may last through the night, but joy comes with the morning.

Psalm 30:5 NLT

The Lord takes pleasure in His people; He adorns the humble with salvation. Let the godly exult in glory; let them sing for joy on their beds. Let the high praises of God be in their throats.

Psalm 149:4-6 ESV

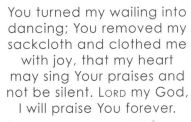

You turned my wailing into
dancing; You removed my
sackcloth and clothed me
with joy, that my heart
may sing Your praises and
not be silent. Lord my God,
I will praise You forever.

Psalm 30:11-12 NIV

Delight yourself in the
Lord and He will give you
the desires of your heart.

Psalm 37:4 NIV

The precepts of the Lord
are right, giving joy to the heart.
The commands of the Lord are
radiant, giving light to the eyes.

Psalm 19:8 NIV

*The prospect
of the righteous is
joy, but the hopes
of the wicked come
to nothing.*

Proverbs 10:28 NIV

His unfailing love

For God so loved the world that
He gave His one and only Son,
that whoever believes in Him shall
not perish but have eternal life.

John 3:16 NIV

God demonstrates His own love
toward us, in that while we were
still sinners, Christ died for us.

Romans 5:8 NKJV

The LORD says, "I have loved you
with an everlasting love; I have
drawn you with unfailing kindness."

Jeremiah 31:3 NIV

Your love, LORD, reaches to the
heavens, Your faithfulness to
the skies. Your righteousness is
like the highest mountains, Your
justice like the great deep.

Psalm 36:5-6 NIV

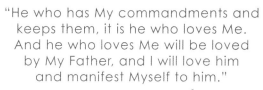

"He who has My commandments and
keeps them, it is he who loves Me.
And he who loves Me will be loved
by My Father, and I will love him
and manifest Myself to him."

John 14:21 NKJV

These three remain: faith, hope and
love. But the greatest of these is love.

1 Corinthians 13:13 NIV

Sow righteousness for yourselves,
reap the fruit of unfailing love.

Hosea 10:12 NIV

Since God loved us that much, we
surely ought to love each other. No
one has ever seen God. But if we love
each other, God lives in us, and His
love is brought to full expression in us.

1 John 4:11-12 NLT

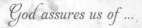

God's love has been poured out into our hearts through the Holy Spirit, who has been given to us.

Romans 5:5 NIV

What great love the Father has lavished on us, that we should be called children of God! And that is what we are!

1 John 3:1 NIV

This is love: not that we loved God, but that He loved us and sent His Son as an atoning sacrifice for our sins.

1 John 4:10 NIV

This is how we know what love is: Jesus Christ laid down His life for us. And we ought to lay down our lives for our brothers and sisters.

1 John 3:16 NIV

"I have loved you even as
the Father has loved Me.
Remain in My love."

John 15:9 NLT

Overwhelming victory is ours
through Christ, who loved us.
And I am convinced that nothing
can ever separate us from
God's love. Neither death nor
life, neither angels nor demons,
neither our fears for today nor
our worries about tomorrow – not
even the powers of hell can
separate us from God's love.
No power in the sky above or
in the earth below – indeed,
nothing in all creation will
ever be able to separate us
from the love of God.

Romans 8:37-39 NLT

"The Father Himself loves you, because you have loved Me, and have believed that I came forth from God."

John 16:27 NKJV

Bundles of blessings

A faithful person will be
richly blessed.

Proverbs 28:20 NIV

The blessing of the Lord
makes one rich, and He
adds no sorrow with it.

Proverbs 10:22 NKJV

Blessings crown the head of the
righteous, but violence overwhelms
the mouth of the wicked. The name
of the righteous is used in blessings,
but the name of the wicked will rot.

Proverbs 10:6-7 NIV

The Lord has remembered us;
He will bless us; He will bless
those who fear the Lord, both
the small and the great.

Psalm 115:12-13 ESV

Jesus replied, "Blessed are
those who hear the word
of God and obey it."

Luke 11:28 NIV

"Blessed are the pure in heart,
for they will see God. Blessed
are the peacemakers, for they
will be called children of God."

Matthew 5:8-9 NIV

Blessed are those whose ways
are blameless, who walk according
to the law of the LORD. Blessed are
those who keep His statutes and
seek Him with all their heart.

Psalm 119:1-2 NIV

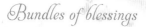

Taste and see that the LORD is good; blessed is the one who takes refuge in Him. Fear the LORD, you His holy people, for those who fear Him lack nothing.

Psalm 34:8-9 NIV

The LORD is my chosen portion and my cup; You hold my lot. The lines have fallen for me in pleasant places; indeed, I have a beautiful inheritance.

Psalm 16:5-6 ESV

"Blessed are the meek, for they will inherit the earth. Blessed are those who hunger and thirst for righteousness, for they will be filled. Blessed are the merciful, for they will be shown mercy."

Matthew 5:5-7 NIV

The LORD will open the
heavens, the storehouse
of His bounty, to send
rain on your land in
season and to bless all
the work of your hands.

Deuteronomy 28:12 NIV

"Blessed are those who
are persecuted because
of righteousness, for theirs is
the kingdom of heaven."

Matthew 5:10 NIV

The Lord will
indeed give what
is good, and our
land will yield
its harvest.

Psalm 85:12 NIV

God assures us of ...

His shield
of protection

The LORD is close to all who
call on Him, yes, to all who call
on Him in truth. He grants the
desires of those who fear Him;
He hears their cries for help
and rescues them. The LORD
protects all those who love Him.

Psalm 145:18-20 NLT

I lift up my eyes to the hills.
From where does my help come?
My help comes from the LORD,
who made heaven and earth.
He will not let your foot be moved;
He who keeps you will not slumber.
Behold, He who keeps Israel will
neither slumber nor sleep. The
LORD is your keeper; the LORD is
your shade on your right hand.

Psalm 121:1-5 ESV

The Lord says, "I will rescue those who love Me. I will protect those who trust in My name. When they call on Me, I will answer; I will be with them in trouble. I will rescue and honor them."

Psalm 91:14-15 NLT

Let the beloved of the Lord rest secure in Him, for He shields him all day long, and the one the Lord loves rests between His shoulders.

Deuteronomy 33:12 NIV

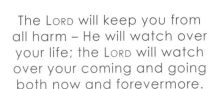

The Lord will keep you from all harm – He will watch over your life; the Lord will watch over your coming and going both now and forevermore.

Psalm 121:7-8 NIV

God's way is perfect. All the Lord's promises prove true. He is a shield for all who look to Him for protection.

Psalm 18:30 NLT

You are my hiding place; You will protect me from trouble and surround me with songs of deliverance.

Psalm 32:7 NIV

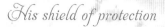

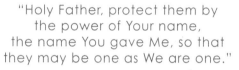

"Holy Father, protect them by
the power of Your name,
the name You gave Me, so that
they may be one as We are one."

John 17:11 NIV

The LORD bless and keep you.

Numbers 6:24 NKJV

Having hope will give you courage.
You will be protected and will rest
in safety. You will lie down unafraid,
and many will look to you for help.

Job 11:18-19 NLT

If you make the
Lord your refuge,
if you make the Most
High your shelter,
no evil will conquer you.
For He will order
His angels to protect
you wherever you go.

Psalm 91:9-11 NLT

God assures us of ...

The gift of grace

Preparing your minds for action,
and being sober-minded, set
your hope fully on the grace
that will be brought to you at
the revelation of Jesus Christ.

1 Peter 1:13 ESV

To each one of us grace was
given according to the measure
of Christ's gift. Therefore He says:
"When He ascended on high,
He led captivity captive,
and gave gifts to men."

Ephesians 4:7-8 NKJV

Grace and peace be yours in
abundance through the knowledge
of God and of Jesus our Lord.

2 Peter 1:2 NIV

In Him we have redemption
through His blood, the forgiveness
of sins, in accordance with the
riches of God's grace.

Ephesians 1:7 NIV

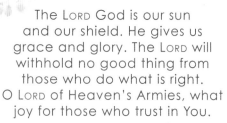

The L‍ord God is our sun
and our shield. He gives us
grace and glory. The L‍ord will
withhold no good thing from
those who do what is right.
O L‍ord of Heaven's Armies, what
joy for those who trust in You.

Psalm 84:11-12 NLT

From His fullness we have all
received, grace upon grace.
For the law was given through
Moses; grace and truth
came through Jesus Christ.

John 1:16-17 ESV

Let us then with confidence draw
near to the throne of grace, that
we may receive mercy and find
grace to help in time of need.

Hebrews 4:16 ESV

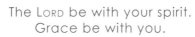

The gift of grace

The Lord be with your spirit.
Grace be with you.

2 Timothy 4:22 NIV

He raised us from the dead
along with Christ and seated
us with Him in the heavenly
realms because we are united
with Christ Jesus. So God can
point to us in all future ages as
examples of the incredible wealth
of His grace and kindness toward
us, as shown in all He has done
for us who are united with
Christ Jesus. God saved you by
His grace when you believed.
And you can't take credit for this;
it is a gift from God. Salvation
is not a reward for the good
things we have done, so none
of us can boast about it.

Ephesians 2:6-9 NLT

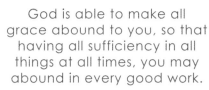

God is able to make all
grace abound to you, so that
having all sufficiency in all
things at all times, you may
abound in every good work.

2 Corinthians 9:8 ESV

Sin shall not have dominion
over you, for you are not
under law but under grace.

Romans 6:14 NIV

I commit you to God and to
the word of His grace, which
can build you up and give
you an inheritance among
all those who are sanctified.

Acts 20:32 NIV

Peace be with you,
dear brothers and
sisters, and may God
the Father and the
Lord Jesus Christ
give you love with
faithfulness.
May God's grace be
eternally upon all
who love our Lord
Jesus Christ.

Ephesians 6:23-24 NLT

His
power to provide

"Your Father knows what you
need before you ask Him."

Matthew 6:8 NIV

God will meet all your needs
according to the riches of His glory
in Christ Jesus. To our God and
Father be glory for ever and ever.

Philippians 4:19-20 NIV

"Why worry about your clothing?
Look at the lilies of the field and
how they grow. They don't work
or make their clothing, yet
Solomon in all his glory was not
dressed as beautifully as they are.
And if God cares so wonderfully
for wildflowers that are here today
and thrown into the fire tomorrow,
He will certainly care for you."

Matthew 6:28-30 NLT

The LORD is my shepherd;
I shall not want.

Psalm 23:1 ESV

"Therefore I tell you, do not worry about your life, what you will eat or drink; or about your body, what you will wear. Is not life more than food, and the body more than clothes? Look at the birds of the air; they do not sow or reap or store away in barns, and yet your heavenly Father feeds them. Are you not much more valuable than they?"

Matthew 6:25-26 NIV

The Lord says, "Give, and it will be given to you. A good measure, pressed down, shaken together and running over, will be poured into your lap. For with the measure you use, it will be measured to you."

Luke 6:38 NIV

63

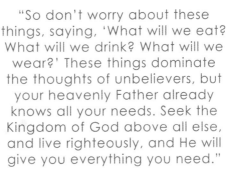

"So don't worry about these things, saying, 'What will we eat? What will we drink? What will we wear?' These things dominate the thoughts of unbelievers, but your heavenly Father already knows all your needs. Seek the Kingdom of God above all else, and live righteously, and He will give you everything you need."

Matthew 6:31-33 NLT

As for the rich in this present age, charge them not to be haughty, nor to set their hopes on the uncertainty of riches, but on God, who richly provides us with everything to enjoy.

1 Timothy 6:17 ESV

The L ORD says, "I will answer
them before they even call
to Me. While they are still talking
about their needs, I will go ahead
and answer their prayers!"

Isaiah 65:24 NLT

The eyes of all look expectantly
to You, and You give them their
food in due season. You open
Your hand and satisfy the
desire of every living thing.

Psalm 145:15-16 NKJV

"Bring all the tithes into the
storehouse so there will be
enough food. If you do," says
the L ORD, "I will pour out a
blessing so great you won't
have enough room to take it in."

Malachi 3:10 NLT

65

His divine power
has given us everything
we need for a godly
life through our
knowledge of Him
who called us by
His own glory
and goodness.

2 Peter 1:3 NIV

A life with Him

God has given us eternal life,
and this life is in His Son.
He who has the Son has life;
he who does not have the
Son of God does not have life.

1 John 5:11-12 NKJV

"This is the will of God, that I
should not lose even one of
all those He has given Me,
but that I should raise them up
at the last day. For it is My
Father's will that all who see
His Son and believe in Him
should have eternal life. I will
raise them up at the last day."

John 6:39-40 NLT

God is so rich in mercy,
and He loved us so much
that even though we were
dead because of our sins,
He gave us life when He
raised Christ from the dead.

Ephesians 2:4-5 NLT

67

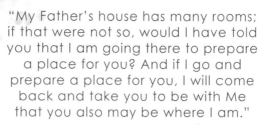

"My Father's house has many rooms; if that were not so, would I have told you that I am going there to prepare a place for you? And if I go and prepare a place for you, I will come back and take you to be with Me that you also may be where I am."

John 14:2-3 NIV

The Scriptures say, "No eye has seen, no ear has heard, and no mind has imagined what God has prepared for those who love Him."

1 Corinthians 2:9 NLT

"Those who find Me find life and receive favor from the Lᴏʀᴅ. But those who fail to find me harm themselves; all who hate me love death."

Proverbs 8:35-36 NIV

"My sheep hear My voice,
and I know them, and they
follow Me. I give them
eternal life, and they will
never perish, and no one will
snatch them out of My hand."

John 10:27-28 ESV

Jesus declared, "I am the Bread
of Life. Whoever comes to Me will
never go hungry, and whoever
believes in Me will never be thirsty."

John 6:35 NIV

"I tell you the truth, those
who listen to My message
and believe in God who sent
Me have eternal life. They will
never be condemned for
their sins, but they have already
passed from death into life."

John 5:24 NLT

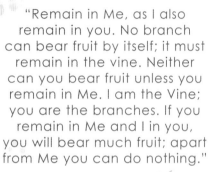

"Remain in Me, as I also remain in you. No branch can bear fruit by itself; it must remain in the vine. Neither can you bear fruit unless you remain in Me. I am the Vine; you are the branches. If you remain in Me and I in you, you will bear much fruit; apart from Me you can do nothing."

John 15:4-5 NIV

God will give you a grand entrance into the eternal Kingdom of our Lord and Savior Jesus Christ.

2 Peter 1:11 NLT

This world is not our permanent home; we are looking forward to a home yet to come.

Hebrews 13:14 NLT

The Father loves
His Son and has
put everything
into His hands.
And anyone who
believes in God's
Son has eternal life.

John 3:35-36 NLT

Trust in the Lord

We are citizens of heaven,
where the Lord Jesus Christ lives.
And we are eagerly waiting for
Him to return as our Savior. He will
take our weak mortal bodies and
change them into glorious bodies
like His own, using the same
power with which He will bring
everything under His control.

Philippians 3:20-21 NLT

Since you have been raised
to new life with Christ, set your
sights on the realities of heaven,
where Christ sits in the place of
honor at God's right hand.
Think about the things of heaven,
not the things of earth. For you
died to this life, and your real
life is hidden with Christ in God.

Colossians 3:1-3 NLT

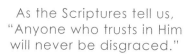

As the Scriptures tell us,
"Anyone who trusts in Him
will never be disgraced."

Romans 10:11 NLT

You keep him in perfect peace
whose mind is stayed on You,
because he trusts in You. Trust in
the Lᴏʀᴅ forever, for the Lᴏʀᴅ
God is an everlasting rock.

Isaiah 26:3-4 ESV

The Lᴏʀᴅ says, "Do not let your
hearts be troubled. You believe
in God; believe also in Me."

John 14:1 NIV

The Lᴏʀᴅ is good, a refuge in
times of trouble. He cares
for those who trust in Him.

Nahum 1:7 NIV

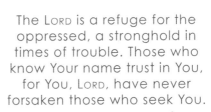

The LORD is a refuge for the oppressed, a stronghold in times of trouble. Those who know Your name trust in You, for You, LORD, have never forsaken those who seek You.

Psalm 9:9-10 NIV

Trust in the LORD with all your heart and lean not on your own understanding.

Proverbs 3:5 NIV

If we are faithful to the end, trusting God just as firmly as when we first believed, we will share in all that belongs to Christ.

Hebrews 3:14 NLT

Trust in Him at all times, O people;
pour out your heart before
Him; God is a refuge for us.

Psalm 62:8 ESV

Yes, the LORD is for me;
He will help me. I will look in
triumph at those who hate me.
It is better to take refuge in
the LORD than to trust in people.
It is better to take refuge in the
LORD than to trust in princes.

Psalm 118:7-9 NLT

May the God of hope fill
you with all joy and peace
as you trust in Him, so that
you may overflow with hope
by the power of the Holy Spirit.

Romans 15:13 NIV

Many sorrows come to the wicked, but unfailing love surrounds those who trust the Lord.

Psalm 32:10 NLT

Keep a firm
foundation of faith

"I tell you the truth, if you
had faith even as small as
a mustard seed, you could
say to this mountain,
'Move from here to there,'
and it would move. Nothing
would be impossible."

Matthew 17:20 NLT

Jesus answered, "The work
of God is this: to believe in
the One He has sent."

John 6:29 NIV

Jesus said, "All things are possible
for one who believes."

Mark 9:23 ESV

Then Jesus told them, "I tell you
the truth, if you have faith and
don't doubt, you can do things
like this and much more."

Matthew 21:21 NLT

77

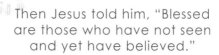

Then Jesus told him, "Blessed are those who have not seen and yet have believed."

John 20:29 NIV

Make every effort to supplement your faith with virtue, and virtue with knowledge, and knowledge with self-control, and self-control with steadfastness, and steadfastness with godliness, and godliness with brotherly affection, and brotherly affection with love.

2 Peter 1:5-7 ESV

Be on your guard; stand firm in the faith; be courageous; be strong. Do everything in love.

1 Corinthians 16:13-14 NIV

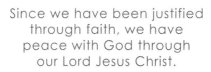

Since we have been justified
through faith, we have
peace with God through
our Lord Jesus Christ.

Romans 5:1 NIV

When your faith remains
strong through many trials,
it will bring you much praise
and glory and honor on the
day when Jesus Christ is
revealed to the whole world.

1 Peter 1:7 NLT

In the gospel the righteousness of
God is revealed – a righteousness
that is by faith from first to last,
just as it is written: "The
righteous will live by faith."

Romans 1:17 NIV

"Believe in the Lord Jesus and you will be saved, along with everyone in your household."

Acts 16:31 NLT

Because of Christ and our faith in Him, we can now come boldly and confidently into God's presence.

Ephesians 3:12 NLT

The Son of Man must be lifted up, that everyone who believes in Him may have eternal life.

John 3:14-15 NIV

Jesus said, "Don't be afraid; just believe."

Mark 5:36 NIV

Build each other up in your most holy faith ...
And show mercy to those whose faith is wavering.

Jude 20, 22 NLT

Live prayerful lives

The LORD says, "Whatever you ask in My name, that I will do, that the Father may be glorified in the Son. If you ask anything in My name, I will do it."

John 14:13-14 NKJV

The eyes of the Lord are on the righteous and His ears are attentive to their prayer, but the face of the Lord is against those who do evil.

1 Peter 3:12 NIV

"Therefore I tell you, whatever you ask for in prayer, believe that you have received it, and it will be yours. And when you stand praying, if you hold anything against anyone, forgive them, so that your Father in heaven may forgive you your sins."

Mark 11:24-25 NIV

82

"Ask and it will be given to you; seek and you will find; knock and the door will be opened to you. For everyone who asks receives; the one who seeks finds; and to the one who knocks, the door will be opened."

Matthew 7:7-8 NIV

The LORD says, "You will call on Me and come and pray to Me, and I will listen to you. You will seek Me and find Me when you seek Me with all your heart."

Jeremiah 29:12-13 NIV

Pray in the Spirit on all occasions with all kinds of prayers and requests. With this in mind, be alert and always keep on praying for all the LORD's people.

Ephesians 6:18 NIV

"When you pray, go into your room, close the door and pray to your Father, who is unseen. Then your Father, who sees what is done in secret, will reward you."

Matthew 6:6 NIV

Do not be anxious about anything, but in every situation, by prayer and petition, with thanksgiving, present your requests to God. And the peace of God, which transcends all understanding, will guard your hearts and your minds in Christ Jesus.

Philippians 4:6-7 NIV

Seek the Lord while you can find Him. Call on Him now while He is near.

Isaiah 55:6 NLT

This is what the LORD says, He who made the earth, the LORD who formed it and established it – the LORD is His name: "Call to Me and I will answer you and tell you great and unsearchable things you do not know."

Jeremiah 33:2-3 NIV

The LORD detests the sacrifice of the wicked, but He delights in the prayers of the upright.

Proverbs 15:8 NLT

The Spirit helps us in our weakness. We do not know what we ought to pray for, but the Spirit Himself intercedes for us through wordless groans.

Romans 8:26 NIV

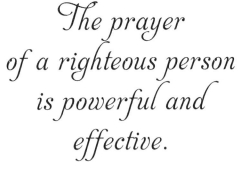

*The prayer
of a righteous person
is powerful and
effective.*

James 5:16 NIV

As for me and my household, we will ...

Fill our
home with worship

Let us worship and bow down;
let us kneel before the Lᴏʀᴅ,
our Maker! For He is our God,
and we are the people of His
pasture, and the sheep of His hand.

Psalm 95:6-7 ESV

Give to the Lᴏʀᴅ the glory due His
name; bring an offering, and
come before Him. Oh, worship
the Lᴏʀᴅ in the beauty of holiness!

1 Chronicles 16:29 NKJV

Since we are receiving a
Kingdom that is unshakable,
let us be thankful and please
God by worshiping Him with
holy fear and awe.

Hebrews 12:28 NLT

Exalt the Lᴏʀᴅ our God; worship
at His footstool! Holy is He!

Psalm 99:5 ESV

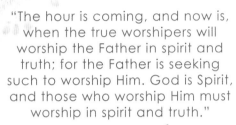

"The hour is coming, and now is, when the true worshipers will worship the Father in spirit and truth; for the Father is seeking such to worship Him. God is Spirit, and those who worship Him must worship in spirit and truth."

John 4:23-24 NKJV

Sing to the Lᴏʀᴅ, for He has done excellent things; this is known in all the earth. Cry out and shout, O inhabitant of Zion, for great is the Holy One of Israel in your midst!

Isaiah 12:5-6 NKJV

Everything on earth will worship You; they will sing Your praises, shouting Your name in glorious songs. Come and see what our God has done, what awesome miracles He performs for people!

Psalm 66:4-5 NLT

I will praise You with my
whole heart; before the gods
I will sing praises to You. I will
worship toward Your holy temple,
and praise Your name for Your
lovingkindness and Your truth;
for You have magnified Your
word above all Your name.

Psalm 138:1-2 NKJV

Let us go to His dwelling place,
let us worship at His footstool,
saying, "Arise, Lord, and come
to Your resting place, You and
the ark of Your might."

Psalm 132:7-8 NIV

The Lord says, "For where
two or three are gathered
together in My name, I am
there in the midst of them."

Matthew 18:20 NKJV

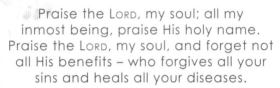

Praise the LORD, my soul; all my inmost being, praise His holy name. Praise the LORD, my soul, and forget not all His benefits – who forgives all your sins and heals all your diseases.

Psalm 103:1-3 NIV

Sing to the LORD a new song; sing to the LORD, all the earth. Sing to the LORD, praise His name; proclaim His salvation day after day.

Psalm 96:1-2 NIV

My mouth is filled with Your praise, declaring Your splendor all day long.

Psalm 71:8 NIV

Praise the LORD. Sing to the LORD a new song, His praise in the assembly of His faithful people.

Psalm 149:1 NIV

Exalt the Lord our God, and worship at His holy mountain; for the Lord our God is holy!

Psalm 99:9 ESV

Discipline our children in the ways of the Lord

Direct your children onto the
right path, and when they are
older, they will not leave it.

Proverbs 22:6 NLT

All your children will be taught
by the LORD, and great will be
their peace. In righteousness
you will be established.

Isaiah 54:13-14 NIV

Do not provoke your
children to anger, but bring
them up in the discipline
and instruction of the Lord.

Ephesians 6:4 ESV

No discipline is enjoyable while it
is happening – it's painful! But
afterward there will be a peaceful
harvest of right living for those
who are trained in this way.

Hebrews 12:11 NLT

Discipline our children in the ways of the Lord

Whoever spares the rod
hates their children, but the
one who loves their children
is careful to discipline them.

Proverbs 13:24 NIV

Blessed is the one whom
God corrects; so do not despise
the discipline of the Almighty.

Job 5:17 NIV

To discipline a child produces
wisdom, but a mother is disgraced
by an undisciplined child.

Proverbs 29:15 NLT

Discipline your children, and they
will give you peace; they will
bring you the delights you desire.

Proverbs 29:17 NIV

Do not provoke your children,
lest they become discouraged.

Colossians 3:21 ESV

Foolishness is bound up in the
heart of a child; the rod of
correction will drive it far from him.

Proverbs 22:15 NKJV

My child, don't reject the
LORD's discipline, and don't be
upset when He corrects you.
For the LORD corrects those He
loves, just as a father corrects
a child in whom he delights.

Proverbs 3:11-12 NLT

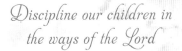

Whoever loves instruction loves knowledge, but he who hates correction is stupid.

Proverbs 12:1 NKJV

Keep your father's commandment, and forsake not your mother's teaching. Bind them on your heart always; tie them around your neck. When you walk, they will lead you; when you lie down, they will watch over you; and when you awake, they will talk with you. For the commandment is a lamp and the teaching a light, and the reproofs of discipline are the way of life.

Proverbs 6:20-23 ESV

Joyful are those
You discipline, Lord,
those You teach with
Your instructions.
You give them relief
from troubled times.

Psalm 94:12-13 NLT

For God's faithful promises we ...

Praise His holy name

I will give thanks to the Lord
because of His righteousness;
I will sing the praises of the
name of the Lord Most High.

Psalm 7:17 NIV

There is none like You, O Lord;
You are great, and Your name
is great in might. Who would
not fear You, O King of the
nations? For this is Your due;
for among all the wise ones
of the nations and in all their
kingdoms there is none like You.

Jeremiah 10:6-7 ESV

Praise Him, you highest
heavens, and you waters above
the heavens! Let them praise
the name of the Lord! For He
commanded and they were
created. And He established
them forever and ever.

Psalm 148:4-6 ESV

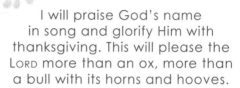

I will praise God's name
in song and glorify Him with
thanksgiving. This will please the
Lord more than an ox, more than
a bull with its horns and hooves.

Psalm 69:30-31 NIV

Praise the Lord, you His servants;
praise the name of the Lord. Let
the name of the Lord be praised,
both now and forevermore.
From the rising of the sun to the
place where it sets, the name
of the Lord is to be praised.

Psalm 113:1-3 NIV

Sing to God, sing in praise of
His name. Rejoice before
Him – His name is the Lord.

Psalm 68:4 NIV

Praise the LORD! Praise the name of the LORD! Praise Him, you who serve the LORD, you who serve in the house of the LORD, in the courts of the house of our God. Praise the LORD, for the LORD is good; celebrate His lovely name with music.

Psalm 135:1-3 NLT

Through Jesus, therefore, let us continually offer to God a sacrifice of praise – the fruit of lips that openly profess His name.

Hebrews 13:15 NIV

Wealth and honor come from You; You are the ruler of all things. In Your hands are strength and power to exalt and give strength to all. Now, our God, we give You thanks, and praise Your glorious name.

1 Chronicles 29:12-13 NIV

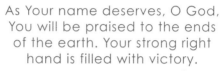

As Your name deserves, O God,
You will be praised to the ends
of the earth. Your strong right
hand is filled with victory.

Psalm 48:10 NLT

I will praise the LORD, and may
everyone on earth bless His
holy name forever and ever.

Psalm 145:21 NLT

The LORD reigns; let the peoples
tremble! He dwells between the
cherubim; let the earth be moved!
The LORD is great in Zion, and He
is high above all the peoples.
Let them praise Your great and
awesome name – He is holy.

Psalm 99:1-3 NKJV

*Let them all praise
the name of the Lord.
For His name is
very great; His glory
towers over the earth
and heaven!*

Psalm 148:13 NLT

Kneel before Him with hearts of thanksgiving

Enter His gates with thanksgiving;
go into His courts with praise. Give
thanks to Him and praise His name.

Psalm 100:4 NLT

With a freewill offering I will
sacrifice to You; I will give thanks
to Your name, O LORD, for it is good.
For He has delivered me from every
trouble, and my eye has looked
in triumph on my enemies.

Psalm 54:6-7 ESV

We thank You, O God!
We give thanks because You
are near. People everywhere
tell of Your wonderful deeds.

Psalm 75:1 NLT

I will thank the LORD with all
my heart as I meet with His
godly people. How amazing
are the deeds of the LORD!

Psalm 111:1-2 NLT

Sing and make music from your heart to the Lord, always giving thanks to God the Father for everything, in the name of our Lord Jesus Christ.

Ephesians 5:19-20 NIV

It is good to praise the LORD and make music to Your name, O Most High, proclaiming Your love in the morning and Your faithfulness at night, to the music of the ten-stringed lyre and the melody of the harp.

Psalm 92:1-3 NIV

Thanks be to God, who always leads us in Christ's triumphal procession and uses us to spread the aroma of the knowledge of Him everywhere.

2 Corinthians 2:14 NIV

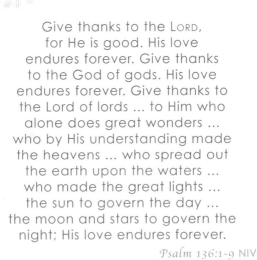

Give thanks to the LORD,
for He is good. His love
endures forever. Give thanks
to the God of gods. His love
endures forever. Give thanks to
the Lord of lords ... to Him who
alone does great wonders ...
who by His understanding made
the heavens ... who spread out
the earth upon the waters ...
who made the great lights ...
the sun to govern the day ...
the moon and stars to govern the
night; His love endures forever.

Psalm 136:1-9 NIV

I will give You thanks, for You answered
me; You have become my salvation.

Psalm 118:21 NIV

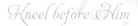

May you be filled with joy,
always thanking the Father.
He has enabled you to share in
the inheritance that belongs to
His people, who live in the light.

Colossians 1:11-12 NLT

Give thanks to the Lord, for He is good;
His love endures forever.

Psalm 107:1 NIV

Sing out your thanks to the Lord;
sing praises to our God with a harp.

Psalm 147:7 NLT

I will give repeated thanks to the Lord,
praising Him to everyone. For He stands
beside the needy, ready to save them
from those who condemn them.

Psalm 109:30-31 NLT

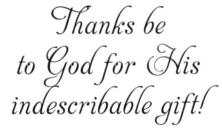

*Thanks be
to God for His
indescribable gift!*

2 Corinthians 9:15 NIV

Rejoice in the Lord

Rejoice in the Lord always.
I will say it again: Rejoice!

Philippians 4:4 NIV

My heart rejoices in the LORD.
In the LORD my horn is lifted high.
My mouth boasts over my enemies,
for I delight in Your deliverance.
There is no one holy like the LORD;
there is no one besides You;
there is no Rock like our God.

1 Samuel 2:1-2 NIV

Rejoice in the LORD and be
glad, you righteous; sing, all
you who are upright in heart!

Psalm 32:11 NIV

The LORD says, "Rejoice because
your names are written in heaven."

Luke 10:20 NKJV

Rejoice always, pray
continually, give thanks in all
circumstances; for this is God's
will for you in Christ Jesus.

1 Thessalonians 5:16-18 NIV

Rejoice! Shout in triumph!
Look, your King is coming to you.
He is righteous and victorious, yet
He is humble, riding on a donkey –
riding on a donkey's colt.

Zechariah 9:9 NLT

May the righteous be glad
and rejoice before God; may
they be happy and joyful.

Psalm 68:3 NIV

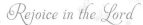

In Him our hearts rejoice,
for we trust in His holy name.
May Your unfailing love
be with us, LORD, even as
we put our hope in You.

Psalm 33:21-22 NIV

Let all those who seek You rejoice
and be glad in You; let such as
love Your salvation say continually,
"The LORD be magnified!"

Psalm 40:16 NKJV

How my spirit rejoices in
God my Savior!

Luke 1:47 NLT

Serve the LORD with reverent fear,
and rejoice with trembling.

Psalm 2:11 NLT

I trust in Your unfailing love.
I will rejoice because You have
rescued me. I will sing to the LORD
because He is good to me.

Psalm 13:5-6 NLT

I know the LORD is always with
me. I will not be shaken, for He
is right beside me. No wonder
my heart is glad, and I rejoice.
My body rests in safety.

Psalm 16:8-9 NLT

All who seek the LORD will
praise Him. Their hearts will
rejoice with everlasting joy.

Psalm 22:26 NLT

Rejoice
with those
who rejoice.

Romans 12:15 NIV

For God's faithful promises we ...

Share our joy with others

Shout joyful praises to God,
all the earth! Sing about the
glory of His name! Tell the
world how glorious He is.

Psalm 66:1-2 NLT

For this, O Lord, I will praise
You among the nations;
I will sing praises to Your
name. You show unfailing
love to Your anointed.

2 Samuel 22:50-51 NLT

Give thanks to the Lord and
proclaim His greatness. Let the
whole world know what He has
done. Tell everyone about His
wonderful deeds. Exult in His holy
name; rejoice, you who worship
the Lord. Search for the Lord and
for His strength; continually seek
Him. Remember the wonders He
has performed, His miracles,
and the rulings He has given.

1 Chronicles 16:8-12 NLT

112

Share our joy with others

I will make Your name to be
remembered in all generations;
therefore the people shall
praise You forever and ever.

Psalm 45:17 NKJV

Oh, give thanks to the LORD!
Call upon His name; make known
His deeds among the peoples!
Sing to Him, sing psalms to Him;
talk of all His wondrous works!

Psalm 105:1-2 NKJV

My mouth will tell of Your
righteous deeds, of Your saving
acts all day long – though I
know not how to relate them
all. I will come and proclaim
Your mighty acts, Sovereign
LORD; I will proclaim Your
righteous deeds, Yours alone.

Psalm 71:15-16 NIV

113

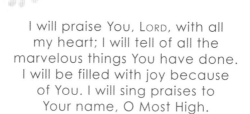

I will praise You, LORD, with all
my heart; I will tell of all the
marvelous things You have done.
I will be filled with joy because
of You. I will sing praises to
Your name, O Most High.

Psalm 9:1-2 NLT

The heavens proclaim the
glory of God. The skies display
His craftsmanship. Day after
day they continue to speak;
night after night they make Him
known. They speak without a
sound or word; their voice is
never heard. Yet their message
has gone throughout the earth,
and their words to all the world.

Psalm 19:1-4 NLT

I will praise the LORD at
all times. I will constantly
speak His praises. I will boast
only in the LORD; let all who are
helpless take heart. Come, let
us tell of the LORD's greatness;
let us exalt His name together.

Psalm 34:1-3 NLT

I come to Your altar, O LORD,
singing a song of thanksgiving
and telling of all Your wonders.

Psalm 26:6-7 NLT

In God we boast all day long,
and praise Your name forever.

Psalm 44:8 NKJV

Sing praises to the Lord. Tell the world about His unforgettable deeds.

Psalm 9:11 NLT

Praise the Lord!

O LORD, our Lord, Your majestic name fills the earth! Your glory is higher than the heavens. You have taught children and infants to tell of Your strength, silencing Your enemies and all who oppose You. When I look at the night sky and see the work of Your fingers – the moon and the stars You set in place – what are mere mortals that You should think about them, human beings that You should care for them? Yet You made them only a little lower than God and crowned them with glory and honor. You gave them charge of everything You made, putting all things under their authority – the flocks and the herds and all the wild animals, the birds in the sky, the fish in the sea, and everything that swims the ocean currents. O LORD, our Lord, Your majestic name fills the earth!

Psalm 8 NLT

117

Lord,
there is no one like You!
For You are great, and
Your name is full of power.
Who would not fear You,
O King of nations?
That title belongs to You alone!
Among all the wise people of the
earth and in all the kingdoms of the
world, there is no one like You.
The Lord is the only true God.
He is the living God and
the everlasting King!

Jeremiah 10:6-7, 10 NLT

O Lord, please guide me

To You, O LORD, I lift up my soul.
O my God, in You I trust;
let me not be put to shame;
let not my enemies exult over
me. Indeed, none who wait
for You shall be put to shame.
Make me to know Your ways,
O LORD; teach me Your paths.
Lead me in Your truth and teach
me, for You are the God of my
salvation; for You I wait all the
day long. Remember Your mercy,
O LORD, and Your steadfast
love, for they have been from
of old. Remember not the sins
of my youth or my transgressions;
according to Your steadfast
love remember me, for the
sake of Your goodness, O LORD!

Psalm 25:1-7 ESV

In the day when I cried out,
You answered me, and made
me bold with strength in my soul.
Though the Lord is on high, yet
He regards the lowly.
Though I walk in the midst of
trouble, You will revive me;
You will stretch out Your hand
against the wrath of my enemies,
and Your right hand will save me.
The Lord will perfect that which
concerns me; Your mercy, O Lord,
endures forever; do not forsake
the works of Your hands.

Psalm 138:3, 6-8 NKJV

A mother's prayers ...

Father of comfort

One thing I ask from the
LORD, this only do I seek: that
I may dwell in the house of
the LORD all the days of
my life, to gaze on the
beauty of the Lord and to
seek Him in His temple. For in
the day of trouble He will
keep me safe in His dwelling;
He will hide me in the shelter
of His sacred tent and set me
high upon a rock. Then my head
will be exalted above the
enemies who surround me; at
His sacred tent I will sacrifice
with shouts of joy; I will sing
and make music to the LORD.
Hear my voice when I call, LORD;
be merciful to me and answer me.
My heart says of You, "Seek
His face!" Your face, LORD, I will
seek. You have been my helper.

Psalm 27:4-9 NIV

I will exalt You, Lord, for You lifted me out of the depths. Lord my God, I called to You for help, and You healed me. To You, Lord, I called; to the Lord I cried for mercy: Hear, Lord, and be merciful to me; Lord, be my help. You turned my wailing into dancing; You removed my sackcloth and clothed me with joy, that my heart may sing Your praises and not be silent. Lord my God, I will praise You forever.

Psalm 30:1-2, 8, 10-12 NIV

Sing of His love

Your love, LORD, reaches to the heavens, Your faithfulness to the skies. Your righteousness is like the highest mountains, Your justice like the great deep. You, LORD, preserve both people and animals. How priceless is Your unfailing love, O God! People take refuge in the shadow of Your wings. They feast on the abundance of Your house; You give them drink from Your river of delights. For with You is the fountain of life; in Your light we see light. Continue Your love to those who know You, Your righteousness to the upright in heart.

Psalm 36:5-10 NIV

123

O God, You are my God;
earnestly I seek You;
my soul thirsts for You;
my flesh faints for You,
as in a dry and weary land
where there is no water.
So I have looked upon You
in the sanctuary, beholding
Your power and glory.
Because Your steadfast love
is better than life, my lips
will praise You.

Psalm 63:1-3 ESV

Gracious blessings

Praise be to the God and
Father of our Lord Jesus Christ,
who has blessed us in the
heavenly realms with every
spiritual blessing in Christ.
For He chose us in Him before
the creation of the world to be
holy and blameless in His sight.
In love He predestined us for
adoption to sonship through
Jesus Christ, in accordance with
His pleasure and will – to the
praise of His glorious grace,
which He has freely given us.

Ephesians 1:3-6 NIV

"I thank You, Father,
Lord of heaven and earth,
that You have hidden
these things from the
wise and understanding
and revealed them
to little children; yes,
Father, for such was
Your gracious will."

Matthew 11:25-26 ESV

A glad heart

My heart is glad and my
tongue rejoices; my body also
will rest secure, because You
will not abandon me to the
realm of the dead, nor will You
let Your faithful one see decay.
You make known to me the path
of life; You will fill me with joy in
Your presence, with eternal
pleasures at Your right hand.

Psalm 16:9-11 NIV

My heart rejoices
in the Lord!
The Lord has made
me strong. Now I
have an answer for
my enemies; I rejoice
because You rescued me.
No one is holy like the
Lord! There is no one
besides You; there is no
Rock like our God.

1 Samuel 2:1-2 NLT